Pocket Guide to IRAN

Instructions for American Servicemen in Iran During World War II

with a new introduction by
STEVEN R. WARD

**Author of Immortal:
A Military History of Iran and Its Armed Forces**

Originally published as
Pocket Guide To Iran
War And Navy Departments
Washington, D.C. 1943

Prepared by
Special Service Division, Services Of Supply
United States Army

Introduction by Steven R. Ward
Copyright © 2012 by Steven R. Ward
All rights reserved.

Except for the introduction, this book is a facsimile of the "Pocket Guide to Iran" prepared in 1943 by the Special Service Division, Services of Supply, United States Army. No copyright is claimed for the text of the "Pocket Guide to Iran." All spellings and punctuation are reproduced as they appear in the original 1943 publication.

ISBN: 1469900718
ISBN 13: 9781469900711

Library of Congress Control Number: 2012900857
CreateSpace, North Charleston, SC

Introduction

By Steven R. Ward

This "pocket guide" for American military personnel was originally written when the United States, more by circumstance than design, was drawn into Iran and into what T.H. Vail Motter, the author of the US Army's official history of its World War II Persian Gulf operations, called "the madhouse of Middle Eastern politics." In straightforward, down-to-earth language these wartime instructions provided an overview of Iranian history and culture that, along with its useful advice on getting along with the Iranians, surely eased America's entry into that country in 1943. What followed was a critically strategic but sometimes tumultuous alliance in oil-rich southwest Asia that, as the guide notes, was even then an important artery of the "world's lifeblood." Since Iran's 1979 Islamic Revolution, however, the relationship has degenerated into mutual hostility and mistrust. Lingering hard feelings contribute to distorted perceptions among Americans about Iran that, too often in our political discourse, feed ideological prejudices and impede rational examination of the best means to serve US national interests. Among these are keeping a region critical to world energy security peaceful and stable. Our interests also require dealing with Iran's continued defiance of international demands for transparency regarding its intentions for acquiring a nuclear weapons capability. Given the state of current US-Iran relations, counsel from the "Greatest Generation" on dealing with Iranians may be constructive and timely.

I say constructive because this pocket guide reminds us of two important but often overlooked bits of history. The first is the story of US-Iranian relations during the war and how these interactions, aided by the forthright advice contained in the guide, might offer lessons for future dealings with Iran. The second is the story of the American servicemen and women of the Persian Gulf Command (PGC), who triumphed over great adversity in Iran to complete a critical World War II mission. Their achievements prompt memories of what Americans can accomplish when they are united and determined, possibly inspiring us to again dare great things in the name of peace and security.

A handbook on Iran was necessary in 1943 because, despite long representation in that country by religious, educational, and philanthropic organizations, Americans at the start of the war were still relative newcomers to the region. Motter wrote that, in the feverish military planning of late 1941, War Department intelligence officers had to turn to the Consultant in Islamic Archaeology at the Library of Congress for information on highways and transportation routes in Iran. According to Joel Sayre, a PGC veteran who in 1945 published his war memoir, *Persian Gulf Command: Some Marvels on the Road to Kazvin,* the initial contingent of troops were elated to discover en route that their destination was Iran and that this was another name for Persia. This delight, based on memories of a Technicolor Persia from the movies, soon dissipated in the reality of Iran, leaving the soldiers feeling seriously betrayed by Hollywood.

The guide's unnamed authors wisely understood that history was important to Iranians and included information on Iran's heritage in the handbook. The writers apparently anticipated that the PGC would have to deal with the past even as the command confronted the stress of working with contemporary Iranians as well as our British and Soviet allies. It is quite likely, however, that the authors did not predict that, according to Sayre, many PGC soldiers would learn to love the country, immersing themselves in Iran's history and culture, learning the language, writing treatises on Iran's heritage, and even composing poetry in Iranian style. Other soldiers, meanwhile, were so enamored of Iran's past glories that they conducted tours of Iranian historical landmarks for their fellow Americans. All noted the Iranians' amazing endurance, widespread artistic skills, thirst for knowledge, cleverness at learning modern techniques, and proud, yet touchy nationalism.

America and Iran Enter the War

The Americans came to Iran uninvited out of necessity and alarm, which meant US-Iranian relations did not begin with a good foundation. Hitler's invasion of the Soviet Union in June 1941 had revived among the Allies the fear of an Axis threat to vital oil fields in Iran and Iraq. Suspicions about Nazi plans were stoked by German victories in North Africa and influence in nearby Syria. Contributing to these worries was Germany's past success using seditious "fifth columns" to infiltrate and dominate Rumania and Bulgaria and to incite a pro-German revolt in Iraq. In the latter country, German intrigues in April 1941 forced London to divert British Indian troops needed elsewhere in the Middle East to restore the Iraqi government. Indeed, Hitler, confident of easy victory over the Soviets, ordered plans for an expedition to march through Iran and capture critical Iraqi and Iranian oil facilities.

In an unintended consequence of earlier American policy, Germany had a presence in Iran and relatively good relations with Iran's ruler, Reza Shah. The Iranians, in large part to offset decades-old Russian and British domination, had first looked to the United States for partnership and help in rebuilding their country after World War I. But, when Washington showed no interest, Reza Shah turned to Germany for assistance. The Iranian leader was a military dictator and admired the Germans, but he was careful to declare his country's neutrality at the war's start in September 1939. The British and Soviets greatly exaggerated the German threat inside Iran; the Allies claimed that as many as 7,000 Germans were in country, but the actual number was closer to 900, only a few of whom were army and intelligence officers working to establish the much feared anti-Allied underground. Reza's secret police limited these Germans' activities, but the Iranian ruler remained reluctant to take any actions, such as expulsions, that could be considered a breach of neutrality and invite German reprisals. Despite Iran's good faith efforts, after Hitler attacked the

Soviets, the Allies set in motion invasion plans to eliminate this feared threat in Iran.

After years of Germany repeatedly seizing the initiative and invading countries to the Allies' detriment, Iran represented, as the guide indicated, the "one time we got there first." Although understandable in the face of Nazi efforts to conquer Europe, London's and Moscow's invasion ignored international law and the immorality of dragging a non-belligerent country into the conflict. Iran had turned to the United States for help in discouraging the imminent aggression but was again disappointed. Iranian diplomats appealed to President Franklin D. Roosevelt using his own words about liberty and self-determination from the Atlantic Charter, which had been announced just eleven days before the Soviet-British invasion. Fearful of the German threat to push through Russia, seize Iranian oil fields, split the British Empire in half, and potentially link up with the Japanese in the Indian Ocean, Washington turned a deaf ear to Iranian pleas.

Starting on August 25, 1941, Soviet forces invaded Iran from the north and British units attacked into western Iran from neighboring Iraq. The Iranian army was outmatched, swiftly defeated, and largely disbanded. Reza Shah accepted the Allies' terms but was unwilling to rule under their political constraints, abdicating instead in favor of his son, Muhammad Reza Shah Pahlavi, who would govern Iran until 1979. Under the pressure of foreign occupation, Iran quickly granted the Allies unrestricted rights to use, maintain, guard, and control all means of transportation and communication in the country.

As critical as the Allies perceived the need to remove the German threat to Iran, it was even more important to secure and strengthen the transport routes across Iran to insure that the Red Army got the supplies it needed to withstand and then defeat the Nazi onslaught. America had initially provided Lend-Lease aid to Great Britain to help fend off the Germans and Italians in North Africa and the Middle East. Following the German attack on the Soviet Union, the program grew to include the delivery of supplies to the Russians through what became known as the "Persian Corridor." To get to the Persian Corridor, American war supplies first had to transit 12,000 miles by sea from the United States around Africa to the Persian Gulf. The limited cargo capacity of the Persian Gulf ports constrained the flow of supplies on this route, but it was the safest for avoiding German U-boats. In addition, with Nazi armies pushing into southern Russia in the late summer of 1941, the Persian Corridor had become the closest route to the main battlefields.

Once the Russian-bound cargoes reached the Iranian and Iraqi ports, this war materiel still had to travel 1,000 miles by rail along a twisting, treacherous path through the Zagros Mountains into central Iran and then back northwest to the Soviet Union. Cargo from Iran's main ports of Khorramshar and Abadan had to cross desert tracks to reach an all-weather road or move by river for transfer to railroad. After the US entered the war in December 1941, the influx of greater amounts of war supplies to meet the Red Army's growing requirements meant that the Persian Gulf ports desperately needed to be enlarged and Iran's railroads and roads had to be expanded and improved to deal with heavier traffic flows. The War Department in Washington rapidly moved into action to deploy the necessary US forces.

The Persian Gulf Command

The enormity of the task ahead strained the War Department's capabilities. Complex issues of allocating appropriately skilled manpower resources and creating a suitable command organization in the middle of wartime mobilization and competing European and Pacific strategic priorities had to be carefully and quickly managed. Despite the difficulties, the War Department by early 1942 succeeded in making America a full partner with Great Britain in expanding the capacity of ports and industrial facilities in Iran. In late 1942 the U.S. military took direct responsibility for the supply effort through Iran with the establishment of the Persian Gulf Command.

Indeed, as Motter relates, supply was the central theme of US Army activity in the Persian Corridor. In his retelling, in this theater the story of the "war of guns" was muted, and military supply, an essential element of victory, took center stage. Sayre noted that the PGC's sole reason for being was to deliver American supplies to the Russians as rapidly as possible in the largest possible quantities. By helping the Soviets stem and then turn back the Nazi tide, the command was earning precious time for the US military to prepare for the invasions of North Africa, Italy, and, ultimately, France.

James Thurber, the American humorist, provided perhaps the best and most succinct descriptions of the PGC's main enemies in this war in his introduction to Sayre's memoirs:

> He [the enemy] didn't come in tanks and war planes, but he contested every foot of the way from the holds of the Liberty ships to the border of Russia, taking mean forms: rain, mud, cold, unbelievable heat, a wicked terrain, bugs, disease, accidents out of the movies, calamities out of the Bible. In the battle of logistics, time is the commander-in-chief of the enemy's forces and holds the center of the line.

There were, of course, "war of guns" dangers and not just from the threat of fifth columnists in Iran. Staging from Eritrea in east Africa, the Italians in 1941 had bombed the island nation of Bahrain, farther south and east in the Persian Gulf. Iran's coast, meanwhile, was in range of Luftwaffe bases in the Mediterranean and, after the German invasion of Russia, in the Caucasus. As the PGC arrived in Iran in late 1942 an Axis radio broadcast jibed, "Ha ha, the Americans are building up the port of Khorramshahr for us to take over."

Thurber also captured the PGC and its supply mission well, describing how the command's railroaders, truckers, road builders, assemblers, and "dock wallopers" (longshoremen or stevedores) unloaded millions of tons of supplies from ships and ran them, one way or another, through Iran to the Russian armies, "hauling, tugging, lifting and shoving" for two years to accomplish the seemingly impossible. The PGC's main missions were construction, signal communications, assembly of trucks and aircraft, and the operation of ports, railways, and truck convoys. Transport was the first among these missions and rail got priority because it could carry larger loads and cargoes than trucks could handle.

INTRODUCTION

The PGC became quite competent at maximizing efficiency, the command's key weapon in the battle against time, backlogs, breakdowns, and weather. Sayre provided this example, incorporating nearly all of the missions, of the command's resourcefulness:

> *The four cases containing a dismembered truck would be fished out of a [ship's] hold down at the port and hauled to an assembly plant; there they would be broken open and the contents would be put together, inspected, and tested. Then the living truck would roll to a dump, be loaded with supplies from the ship that had brought it over dead, and reach Russia before the ship that brought it had left Khorramshahr. By that time the wood of the cases would probably be on the roof of a new wing at the Command hospital.*

Still, as in all wars, mission accomplishment would have been impossible without the steady performance of more routine assignments by the quartermaster troops who ran the depots and operated bakeries, laundries, water supply, refrigerated warehouses, and even ice cream plants. Others, such as medical, dental, and hospital personnel as well as the military police, also played critical roles in taking care of the command's troops and installations.

The PGC's maximum strength, attained in early 1944, was just under 30,000 Americans. It also employed a peak native work force of 42,000 Iranians of various ethnic and tribal backgrounds along with some Poles and Iraqis. Almost 100 percent of the command's railroaders had belonged to this occupation as civilians while the truck regiments were drawn from the ranks of civilian truckers in the United States. War Department policy was that African-Americans should serve in the armed forces in numbers proportionate to the population, so black soldiers constituted roughly 10 percent of PGC strength. The initial deployment plan for the still segregated Army included three Negro port battalions and two Negro engineer dump truck companies. According to Sayre, the PGC had its share of "splendid physical specimens" but some in its ranks were "men of the upper middle years and others whose draft boards should have taken a closer look." This did not prove to be a problem because, as Motter reported one US Army colonel saying, "loneliness and the heat rapidly separated the men from the boys."

Persian Corridor Challenges

The hardships facing the command's personnel were legion. Sayre shared that shortly after arriving the American soldiers began joking that PGC stood for "People Going Crazy." Thurber, meanwhile, imagined a meeting near St. Lo, France, shortly after D-Day, between a captain and a replacement officer from a PGC railroad unit in which the latter introduced himself saying, "Some of the guys in Iran think I was yellow to get myself transferred here."

This was no exaggeration. American railroaders, for example, faced various dangers involving accidents and derailments on the overstressed Iranian rail lines. One of the worst hardships was navigating the roughly 220 tunnels between southwestern Iran and the Russian depots. In one 163-mile-long section there were 133 tunnels totaling 47 miles in length. Because Iranian tunnels were not ventilated the longer passageways filled with steam and often reached temperatures of 180 degrees Fahrenheit. In a move called "charging the rat holes," the American engineers and firemen would try to escape the heat by throttling their trains to a crawl and then, after climbing to the ground, stumbling alongside the locomotives in the dark while clinging to the train's grab irons. Occasional collisions on the busy tracks in the early days of the Military Railway Service fortunately resulted in only a few deaths and injuries, although at times operations had to be restricted to daylight hours to reduce the risks of accidents.

Similar to the railroaders' challenges, PGC truck drivers found navigating Iran's mostly unpaved roads to be an ordeal. US truck convoys wound through deep gorges, rugged mountains, and dangerous switchbacks. The men and vehicles often strained up grades of 10 to 12 percent, and, in winter, through heavy rains and drifting snow with temperatures falling as

INTRODUCTION

low as −25 degrees. During the summer, American teamsters crossed dry hot plains where temperatures reached 120 degrees in the shade and where dust storms and the trucks' own dust plumes choked the drivers. On top of this, the Americans competed with sheep, goats, horses, camels, and unwary Iranians for the right of way, were attacked by armed bandits, and faced the constant danger of accidents on the thousands of curves and steep embankments. Each journey pulverized men's kidneys, left bumps on heads that bounced against cab roofs, and rubbed skin off the small of the drivers' backs. Lower back injuries were common among the drivers, some of whom would steer their trucks from the running boards just to give themselves a chance to stand erect and get some relief from the constant bumpy ride across Iran's potholed roads. The trucks and their vital parts were literally sandblasted by the desert dust storms while bumps tore off gas tanks and tires designed to last eighty thousand miles seldom made it past four thousand.

At the ports the PGC unloaded the Liberty ships using Army port battalions that drew heavily on experienced longshoremen. Sayre noted, however, that "among the Negroes there are many country boys who never even saw a ship before they were drafted, let alone helped unload one." Taking the view that good longshoring is "largely a matter of horse sense," the command was able to conduct virtually continuous stevedoring and lighterage (unloading by barge) operations at Iran's three ports. The US crews competed to make the best ship turnaround times at the ports. While it took the British an average of 55 days to get a ship into a berth, unloaded, and on its way, the US longshoremen dropped the turnaround time to 40 days in June 1943 and then to 8 by September 1944. The PGC battalions became so good at unloading ships that Khorramshahr, at its 1944 peak, was the world's third largest port in terms of tonnage handled.

Through it all there was Iran's unrelenting heat, which left no PGC soldier untouched. Sayre noted that three towns near the main PGC bases in southwestern Iran, in what he described as a topsy-turvy chamber of commerce spirit, claimed to be the hottest places on earth. PGC soldiers, despite penalties for not wearing their dog tags, kept them in shirt pockets

INSTRUCTIONS FOR AMERICAN SERVICEMEN IN IRAN DURING WORLD WAR II

when working in the open to avoid burns from the overheated metal. The command's medics worked hard to keep the heat casualties down by forcing the soldiers to take precautions. But, soldiers being soldiers, some took their chances. In particular, periods of heat and boredom, according to Sayre, often became time for the running of a "perspiration handicap." This competition involved a soldier rolling up a sleeve and bending an elbow to see how fast he could fill an empty C-ration can with sweat (Sayre records that 8 minutes, 41 seconds was the PGC record although he doesn't specify the size of the can).

As mentioned above, the Allied invasion conscripted Iran into the war against the Axis, making the Iranians the fourth partner in the American, British, and Soviet effort to keep the Red Army supplied for the gargantuan struggle against Hitler's war machine. As Motter wrote, "Although [Iran's] sovereignty was reaffirmed... the normal exercise of sovereignty was so circumscribed by the demands of the war as to be virtually suspended for the duration." Motter also eloquently emphasized the American determination to succeed in this mission by creating an early "coalition of the willing":

> *It could not be felt, as a swirling sandstorm is felt; it was not visible as the swarms of stevedores unloading ships, or convoys of trucks creeping through snow-choked mountains. It was a thing as intangible as discouragement, as impalpable as heat. It was a spirit shaped by diplomats and expressed by the sheer obstinacy of men's guts, a spirit animated by Roosevelt, who "considered Iran something of a testing ground for the Atlantic Charter and for the good faith of the United Nations."*

In this regard, the handbook was an important tool for keeping the "Iranis" (the guide's version of "Irani," the Persian word for Iranian) participating in the mission or at least willing to remain passively silent in the face of foreign armies operating in their territory. Such guidance was especially valuable because the stress of the foreign occupation of Iran was at times very severe. The Allies had commandeered much of

Iran's economy along with its transportation system, which upset commerce and created serious food shortages and local famines. Allied spending for goods and services, meanwhile, unleashed a severe inflation (estimated at 900 percent) that was accompanied by speculation, hoarding, and black market operations. In contrast to the general poverty of Iran, American encampments were large and well supplied and, as Motter reported, "muffled booming [was] heard that marked, day after day, the detonation of antipersonnel mines set off by native prowlers attempting the barriers enclosing the foreigners' stores of goods and food."

Despite such problems, the Iranians initially saw the American troops as dynamic, cheerful, and friendly, not aloof like the British or fear-inspiring like the Russians. Most US soldiers apparently followed the handbook's list of do's and don'ts. Incidents of drinking, brawling, and deadly traffic accidents, however, were common and upset the Iranians, who found insult added to injury because U.S. personnel enjoyed *de facto* immunity from prosecution under Iranian law.

The Persian Gulf Command worked hard to make the relationship succeed. For example, no US combat forces or British combat units were available to protect PGC operations and supplies from tribal raids. To enhance security the command adopted a policy of mutual trust rather than force in dealing with the tribes. Friendly negotiations were held with all of the important sheiks and khans. These tribal chiefs ruled thousands of followers and assumed responsibility for enforcing respect for the security of Americans employed constructing highways in isolated areas and for the safety of American convoys, camps, stockpiles, and equipment. Already rich by local standards, the chiefs were paid only a small honorarium, which they accepted proudly as a token of confidence in them by the powerful foreigners. The chiefs also provided local labor, guards and guides, and even local supplies. In an important show of faith, the Americans loaned rifles to the tribes, who, despite the weapons' value, returned them all.

In a less serious but still important example of cooperation, one American captain headed a large anti-malaria army of nearly 2,000 small boys armed with "flit guns" (hand-help pump sprayers named after a popular insecticide). Stalking the mosquitoes all over the coastal districts, the Iranian youngsters lowered the malaria incidence spectacularly, according to Sayre. The boys asked the captain to train them to drill and salute and then proudly performed these military duties.

Working together was not always easy for the Americans and their multiple allies in Iran. One PGC memo for the troops spelled out the command's expectations:

> *This depot is an International Settlement. You will work with… USSR Air Corps, RAF (Royal Air Force), Iranians, Iraqis, Arabians, and Indians. Such success in our work as we have had has been built on the co-operation and mutual understanding of these groups. It is essential that this "good will" be maintained and we count on you to maintain it.*

The Soviets proved to be the most difficult partners. In addition to putting constraints on the presence and activities of US personnel in Soviet-controlled northern Iran, the Russians were especially demanding in their inspection of the vehicles and aircraft produced by the command. Ill feelings occasionally arose when the Soviet inspectors refused to accept equipment with only minor imperfections. The Russians even went so far as to claim that lumber salvaged from the packing cases for the trucks belonged to them. This was a contentious issue because useable wood for construction was always in short supply in Iran. An eventual compromise allowed the Americans to take enough wood to meet many of their pressing construction needs, but the rest was given to the Russians.

Motter and Sayre reported that the native labor posed numerous challenges. In the press of war the unskilled Iranian factory workers had to be taught as they worked, and initial turnover was high. US soldier-instructors mingled throughout the assembly lines and created an efficient labor force marked by generally smooth relations between Americans and natives and between various national and other groups. Over time, the Iranians became skilled factory hands and some even served as supervisors. To combat the inflation unleashed in Iran, the

United States provided housing, mess facilities, and rations for the native workers.

Training Iranian truck drivers proved slightly more difficult. PGC schools graduated more than 7,500 drivers, who learned to drive well enough despite their lack of English. Islamic fatalism, however, led to the drivers' acceptance of crashes as the will of Allah. Inexperience, meanwhile, prompted some to resort to leaping from the cab when facing problems such as failing brakes.

Other problems arose when Iran's many different ethnicities and tribal groups came into contact with one another. In the south, in particular, the antagonism between Arab and Persian workmen was a fairly constant problem. One solution was to place the different groups on separate shifts to avoid confrontations. Managing shifts also helped reduce production slowdowns during the holy month of Ramadan, when many Muslim workers, whose religion required them to do without food and water during daylight, would not report for the day shift. PGC supervisors quickly learned to put Armenian Christians on the day shift and let Muslims work at night after they broke their fast with a large evening meal. The US Army was careful in wartime Iran about religion. Sayre noted that the command's view was that, "Religion is something these people over here don't kid about... We've got enough wars on our hands already without getting mixed up in any holy ones." Not surprisingly, the PGC set out restrictions, such as ordering personnel to remain on post during observances of holy days, to avoid offending Iranians.

The Iranians understandably held some resentment toward the occupying Allies. This caused a rise in pro-German sentiment in some quarters, but the Nazi threat in Iran remained a minor one. There was an increase in fifth column activity in 1943, but by the end of the summer British counterintelligence officers had penetrated the principle German organization and helped the Iranian government arrest most of the suspected or proven Iranian collaborators. Citing these Nazi subversive activities, Iran declared war on Germany in September 1943, which insured the Iranians a place among the United Nations.

PGC Accomplishments

Despite it all, the Persian Gulf Command persevered in its mission and racked up some impressive accomplishments and statistics. Sayre, supported by Motter, rightly claimed that the PGC helped earn precious time for the US military to prepare for combat operations in the European theater, saving an incalculable number of American lives. He also argued, again with much justification, that the PGC should be credited with a colossal assist in the Red Army's destruction of a large part of the German armed forces. There is no question that when the Red Army began its war-winning offensives in 1943 its mobility rested heavily on American vehicles assembled and delivered by the Persian Gulf Command.

In comparison to the 22 million long tons of war materiel landed in Europe for US forces, the United States provided roughly 17 ½ million long tons of supplies to the Soviets between January 1942 and May 1945. Nearly half, about 7.9 million long tons, of the Soviet-bound supplies were discharged at Persian Gulf ports between 1941 and 1945, and 4 million of this was handled by ports operated by the US Army. American forces of the Persian Gulf Command delivered the bulk of these imports, which were estimated as enough to supply 60 Red Army combat divisions. Most of this material was carried by rail, but the total long tons carried by trucks (618,946) represented an essential reserve supply line that filled the gap when no other means were available to meet the urgent need to move supplies to the Russians.

The PGC far exceeded expectations on truck and aircraft production, according to Motter. From early 1942 to September 1945, the United States provided the Soviets with 409,526 trucks, the equivalent of 7 ½ months of the highest annual rate of production achieved by American factories during the war. More important, this amount represented an estimated 2 years and 7 months of Soviet prewar production. Nearly 45% of the Lend-Lease trucks (184,112) reached Russia through the Persian Corridor and 88% of these were assembled in the truck assembly plants in Iran run by PGC ordnance units. The command's vehicles made up fully one-quarter of the Red Army truck fleet.

The PGC also excelled on aircraft production despite the numerous problems caused by the need for skilled technical personnel to handle the complex assembly process. The first American aircraft was delivered in February 1942 and the last few were conveyed to the Russians in May 1945. During the peak year of American deliveries of aircraft to the USSR, the PGC, which produced A-20 support bombers and P-39 and P-40 fighters, accounted for half. Assembly rates rose from an average of 67 aircraft per month in 1942 to roughly 140 aircraft per month in 1944, reaching a temporary peak of 301 aircraft for the month of June 1944. In the end, 4,874 out of 14,834 American aircraft sent to the Soviets under Lend-Lease went through the Persian Gulf.

Other achievements include the expansion of Iran's railroad system with new trunk lines to the ports, the increase and improvement of rolling stock, and the reduction in train accidents from improved track maintenance and upgrades. In October 1941 the Iranian State Railway was capable of carrying only 6,000 tons per month, but two years later its capacity had been increased nearly thirty times to 175,000 tons per month. Signal Corps units of the Persian Gulf Command created, virtually from scratch, a network of instant and reliable communication without which the transport of supplies to the USSR would have been severely handicapped.

Visitor, Doctor, or Inmate

In the preface to his history, Motter, writing in 1951, speculated that the true significance of Persian Corridor operations might not be the aid to Russia and its contribution to victory, but instead would be the intimate association of the United States and Iran. He noted early in his history that a major unasked question at the time of the deployment of US Army units to Iran was "Had America come to the madhouse of Middle Eastern politics as visitor, doctor, or inmate?" During the war, Washington had sent military missions to strengthen Iran's army and security forces, and by war's end, America had committed to Iran's survival as an independent state. Although President Roosevelt had hoped to make Iran an example of Big Three cooperation as an alternative to conflict, it was clear by 1945 that Moscow was aggressively trying to subvert Iran. As Motter was drafting his history, the United States had allied with the Iranians to press the Red Army to withdraw from northern Iran and to foil Soviet attempts, in the first crisis of the Cold War, to break apart Iran by establishing two pro-Soviet republics in Iranian Azerbaijan and Kurdistan. In Motter's view, by undertaking to strengthen Iran the United States became a doctor, but only one who could prescribe and hope for the best.

Motter could not have foreseen how turbulent this relationship would become in the coming years and decades as the United States repeatedly tried to do more than "prescribe and hope for the best." America in 1953 would help overthrow Iran's elected prime minister to keep Muhammad Reza Shah Pahlavi on his throne. Seeing Iran as an important bulwark to Soviet expansionism, Washington supported the growth and modernization of Iran's armed forces, providing a standing military advisory group to help with the effort. In the early 1960s popular Iranian anger at the shah's rule, including his acceptance of a Status of Forces agreement that exempted US personnel in Iran from the Iranian legal system, helped a radical cleric named Ruhollah Khomeini come to prominence. The 1979 Islamic Revolution was, in part, a reaction to the large presence of US nationals supporting the shah's massive military buildup during that decade. After Grand Ayatollah Khomeini replaced the shah as Iran's ruler, the alliance would be shattered, Iran would hold US diplomats and Marines hostage for 444 days, and America would suffer an embarrassing military failure when a hostage rescue attempt would have to be aborted because of equipment breakdowns.

By the early 1980s America clearly was no longer a doctor, and, if not an inmate, then the United States was deeply entangled with Iran in a vicious circle of mutual hostility, distrust, and recrimination. In the three decades following the release of the American hostages in January 1981, Iran has seen itself at war with the United States. In the 1980s, Iran played a role in deadly anti-US terrorism, attacked American-flagged shipping in the Persian Gulf, and foolishly attacked US naval forces, nearly sinking an American frigate with a naval mine in one instance. The United States reciprocated by sinking a large part of the Iranian navy, supporting Iraq in its war against Iran, and enforcing an arms embargo that contributed to Iran's defeat by Iraq in 1988. Tragically, just before that war's end a US Navy warship accidentally shot down an Iranian airliner, killing all 270 crew and passengers.

Washington has continued efforts to contain and weaken Iran through international and unilateral economic sanctions. Iran, fearful that US policies seek regime change, has worked continuously to undermine the US position in the region by alternately trying to court and intimidate its neighbors. The Iranian regime also has sought to disrupt efforts to resolve the conflict between Israel and the Arabs. In the mid-1990s, an Iranian-supported Saudi Shia group attacked US military personnel at the Khobar Towers complex in Saudi Arabia, killing 19 and wounding 372 Americans. Since 2001, Iran has supported Afghan and Iraqi militant groups fighting US forces in those countries. By 2011, the primary source of mutual antipathy centered on issues relating to growing international concerns that the Iranian government was pursuing the development of nuclear weapons along with its indigenous nuclear power capability.

The Guide Today

Nearly seven decades after US troops first deployed to Iran in World War II, the Islamic Republic of Iran poses numerous challenges to the United States. The "intimate association" continues but is more than ever a relationship between enemies. Every US Administration since President Carter has tried without success to resolve the challenges posed by Iran. For this reason alone, it is important all Americans have at least some familiarity with Iran and its people. This pocket guide to Iran still serves as a brief and useful starting point.

As mentioned earlier, the authors of the following instructions to American servicemen recognized that history and culture are extremely important to Iranians. Ambassador John W. Limbert, who was among the US diplomats taken hostage by Iranian revolutionaries in 1979 and later served as the first

Deputy Assistant Secretary of State for Iran from 2009 to 2010, repeated this observation in his recent book, *Negotiating with Iran: Wrestling the Ghosts of History*. Limbert, who speaks fluent Persian and studied and taught in Iran for years prior to joining the State Department in 1973, has written that, while one doesn't need to be a scholar of Iranian history, it is important to be aware of how that history has influenced the Iranians.

This consciousness can be critical in helping comprehend Iranian actions today. Such awareness, as provided by the brief history and practical advice in the handbook, can reduce our reliance on overly simplified Iranian stereotypes and generalizations about this ancient country. In turn, this knowledge can avoid the distorted perceptions and ideological bias that have handicapped efforts to improve relations. This should not be viewed as hopeless because, while the Iranian regime is hostile to the US government, the Iranian people—more than 70 million today as compared to the 15 million citizens at the time the handbook was written—have consistently shown a favorable attitude toward the United States and Americans. Past attempts by both sides to create openings for better relations suggest a common desire to reduce the hostility.

The guide's best and still most applicable advice probably is to treat Iranians well and consider their viewpoints. This is what the Persian Gulf Command did so successfully. As uninvited guests in Iran, US soldiers seemed to intuitively understand that more cooperation was to be gained from the respectful treatment of a people proud of their Persian and Islamic heritages. Friendly acts, the guide noted, may win the Iranians' confidence. The handbook's suggestion that ordinary decency, politeness, and consideration are keys to negotiating the formal ways of the Iranians is something US diplomats in the intervening decades have repeatedly advised. Similarly, toning down rhetoric would be in line with this sage advice from the handbook: "Don't threaten Iranis; use persuasion, explanation, and rewards to get things done." This, of course, does not mean having blind faith in Iranian words and promises. As the guide advises, "Don't mistake courtesy for friendship; an Irani is always polite, but he is fundamentally suspicious of foreigners." A greater American understanding and approval

INTRODUCTION

of such an approach should help fulfill, as Ambassador Limbert has written, one of the first conditions of negotiations: understand the other side's position, even if you don't accept it.

Steven R. Ward is a senior intelligence analyst for the Central Intelligence Agency and is the author of Immortal: A Military History of Iran and Its Armed Forces *(Georgetown University Press, 2009). All statements of fact, opinion, or analysis expressed are those of the author and do not reflect the official positions or views of the CIA or any other U.S. government agency. Nothing in the contents should be construed as asserting or implying U.S. Government authentication of information or Agency endorsement of the author's views.*

Persepolis - Destroyed by Alexander, 331 B.C.

Pocket Guide To Iran

CONTENTS

	PAGE
Introduction	1
Oil—The World's Lifeblood	3
Iran and the War	5
Your Double Part	7
Getting Along in Iran	9
Meet the Iranis	11
The Moslem Religion	15
Irani Customs and Manners	19
Land of Iran	25
History and Government	27
Sanitary Conditions	31
Miscellaneous Information	33
Check List of Do's and Don'ts	36
Hints on Pronouncing Persian	39
List of Most Useful Words and Phrases	43

Introduction

AS AN AMERICAN SOLDIER assigned to duty in Iran (once called Persia), you are undertaking the most important job of your life. There is no other war theater where military success by the United States and her fighting Allies will contribute more to final victory over the Axis.

You've heard a lot of talk in this war about life lines—the sea lanes and land routes by which military supplies flow into the combat zones to be turned against the enemy. Iran is much more than a life line. It is a major source of the power that keeps the United Nations' military machine turning over—oil.

Because of its prime strategic value, Iran is the only country in the world where the armies of three of the United Nations—Great Britain, Russia, and the United States—are operating in daily touch with each other. This combination of great powers, cooperating in the defense of Iran, is a clear-cut indication of the decisive importance of the task you and your outfit have been called upon to do.

INSTRUCTIONS FOR AMERICAN SERVICEMEN IN IRAN DURING WORLD WAR II

You, as an American, have a responsibility that goes beyond the ordinary military duties required of you. Your country has a reputation throughout the world for decency and unselfishness in its dealings with other nations. That reputation is a major asset for us in this global war. By your actions you can uphold it or destroy it. Accordingly, it is part of your job to establish and maintain friendly relations with the soldiers of our Allies—Russia and Great Britain—and with the people of Iran (Iranis). Most of those you meet won't know very much about Americans, except by reputation. They will watch to see how you act and what you do and probably say to themselves: "So, this is what Americans are like." And what they think of us will have much to do with our military success or failure.

It isn't a very difficult job. You'll be expected to act pretty much as you would at home, using your common sense to tell you what to do when you run into a tough situation. You'll be expected to keep your mouth shut and your eyes open even after you are sure of your ground. And you'll need to respect the ways of thinking and doing things of the Iranis and of the British and Russian soldiers, no matter how different they may be from your own. If you adopt the attitude that we Americans don't know all the answers and that the world doesn't revolve around Kankakee, Ill., you won't be very far off the target in your dealings with other peoples.

Beyond a spirit of tolerance and a willingness to meet the other fellow half way, the thing you'll need most in order to get along in Iran is information. Your opinion of the country and the people will never be any better than your knowledge of them. As you exercise your curiosity and gain fresh knowledge, you will increase your efficiency as a soldier and will add personal value and pleasure to a tough job.

This guidebook is to help you move in that direction, but it is little more than a preview. A smart soldier will soon know far more about the country than is to be found between these covers. That is the target to shoot at, and there is no better way to begin getting acquainted with the country than by understanding Iran's present position in this global war.

Oil—The World's Lifeblood

IRAN IS important to the United Nations for a number of reasons. It is the land bridge by which to get supplies to Russia, and it might have become the path over which Hitler's armies could drive into India or to the Red Sea and the Suez Canal. But, more important than anything else, Iran is one of the great power reservoirs of the world. Napoleon once said that an army marches on its stomach. Today armies march on oil. Were all supplies of oil suddenly to vanish, every large industrial nation in the world would collapse almost overnight. Oil is the lifeblood of the modern world.

In that part of the world to which you've been assigned there are two great oil-bearing areas that together constitute the "powerhouse" of the United Nations. The northwest area, stretching between the Araxes River in South Russia to the steppes north of the Caucasus, is the heart of the Soviet Union, measured in terms of barrels of oil. Second only to these oil fields in and around Baku on the Caspian Sea are those in Iran and Iraq, which supply Great Britain and us in the Middle East, North Africa, and on the North Atlantic.

One of the great military thinkers of the present day has said that the quadrangle bounded by the cities of Astrakhan, Teheran, Basra, and Aleppo is the true strategic or power center of the war, "an area in which a German success would mean the almost certain collapse of Russia and the probable collapse of Great Britain as well." Should its occupation lead to a German conquest of the Near East, not only would the British Empire be cut in half, but the prestige of the United

Nations would be radically lowered. Note the names of the cities and then look at the map in the center of this guide.

You will see that you and your fellow soldiers are holding down two sides of the quadrangle. You will continue to hold them down so long as there is unity between the armies of the United Nations in Iran—the unity that comes from mutual confidence and respect. It is familiar strategy of Hitler and his Axis gang to create distrust and doubt between allies and the people friendly to them. You can help defeat that strategy by working to keep the good will of your allied comrades in arms and of the Irani people.

So doing you will become a force in keeping Iran on the Allied side. You will help to keep it open as a channel by which to move lend-lease supplies into Russia. And its annual production of 80,000,000 barrels of oil, originating in the fields near Bandar Shapur and Kermanshah, will continue to supply our tanks and fighting planes in the Middle East and North Africa and to fuel the ships of the British fleet in the Mediterranean and the Indian Ocean.

Iran And The War

FOR ABOUT 3,000 years Iran has been a battleground. Its people took turns in conquering and being conquered. After 3,000 years of it they grew tired of war; they wanted to stay neutral in this war as they did in the last. But that did not suit Hitler's program.

Until he invaded Russia, Hitler's pattern of conquest called for getting the job done in the easiest way. If his propagandists and his "tourists" could demoralize a people and an army, the panzers had an easier job to do. That way it wouldn't cost so much in men or precious material. He tried the same strategy in Iran.

Long before we got into the war, Axis agents had poured into the country. They held key jobs in power companies, in banks, and even in government departments; they infested the towns and cities and worked to stir up the wild tribesmen of the mountain and desert areas.

Hitler's public propagandists, too, were active. The Nazi film "Victory in the West" was shown to capacity crowds in Teheran, the capital city. Nazis subsidized theater managers for using German newsreels. Nazi broadcasters, among other lies, even told the Iranis that Hitler really was a Moslem, related to their great Prophet Mohammed.

It didn't work. After many protests against Nazi activity in the country, the Russians and the British moved in on August 25, 1941. That was one time we got there first. The Shah, Reza Khan, abdicated. His son took over the throne and concluded a treaty with the Allied Nations. Nazi agents who could be found were interned, or fled the country.

Now, with the consent of the Iran Government, troops of the United Nations guard this great land bridge between Europe and Asia, its oil wells and refineries, and the highways and railroads which form the life line to our Russian allies. Our troops are in the minority among these occupying forces. One whole British Army, organized in the summer of 1942, is on duty in this theater. The Russians, reacting to developments north of the Caucasus, have had to lean more and more upon the military establishment in Iran as a prop to the forces operating between the Black Sea and the Caspian. Measured against these responsibilities and undertakings, our own effort in Iran has been relatively limited and we can appropriately be modest about it.

Your Double Part

YOU ENTER Iran not only as a soldier, but also as an individual. That is our strength—if we are smart enough to use it. As a soldier, your duties will be clear-cut. But in a place like Iran, what you do as an individual—on your own—can be almost as important. Iran is a possible trouble spot. A great deal of our success or failure may depend on whether the Iranis like us. If they like us, they can help us in countless ways. If they don't, they can cause us trouble. If they are doubtful, your friendly acts may win their confidence.

Getting Along In Iran

GETTING ALONG in Iran is pretty much like getting along at home, except that the people are more formal. Use ordinary decency, politeness, and consideration, and you won't have trouble. But be a little restrained, though friendly. And remember always that you aren't going to Iran to change or reform the Iranis or to tell them how much better we do things at home. Their ways of doing things have been good enough for them for some thousands of years, and they aren't likely to change because you think they should.

Even with the best will in the world, you can get off on the wrong foot with the Iranis unless you know a few things about them. There are two principal danger points. Their politics and their religion. *Stay out of arguments or discussions of either.* In the first place, you don't know enough about them to have an opinion; in the second place, they aren't your business; in the third place, you can make a lot more friends for our side by just being a decent, ordinary, friendly American.

Meet The Iranis

IN THE cities you will find most of the Iranis friendly to Americans. Iran has often turned for help in her problems to American scientists and economists, and the Iranis appreciate what these Americans have done to help them. They appreciate, too, the efforts of American missionaries to build hospitals and stamp out disease. Quite a few of Iran's professional men, such as doctors, were educated in the United States, and they have brought back favorable reports about us and our country.

In the country districts you will find that the people know less about Americans. Here the German agents have been particularly active and shrewd. Since the native Iranis have a distrust of most foreigners, the Nazis have sent their agents—disguised as natives and well supplied with money—into all sorts of remote places to spread their lies and stir up trouble. (It is believed that at least 100 of these Axis undercover agents are still active in various parts of Iran, in spite of the efforts to weed them out.) Your best way to beat this game is to be friendly and not to offend the Iranis by careless disregard for their customs.

The 15,000,000 Iranis are a mixture of peoples. They belong to the so-called Caucasian race, like ourselves, despite the dark color of the skins of many of them. Today many of them are more westernized than the inhabitants of bordering countries. You will see European costumes quite generally in the cities, but less in the country. One thing nearly all Iranis have in common is the Moslem religion, which we will talk about a little later on.

In the country, most of the people are tenant farmers, and they are very poor. They grow cereals, fruits, cotton, opium, and some vegetables. From one-third to two-thirds of their produce goes to the landlord; they live on the rest. Lack of water for irrigation (only about 10 percent of the land is under cultivation) accounts for much of Iran's poverty. In many districts you will see mounds that look like giant anthills. They are "kanats" which mark wells connected by underground channels through which water is brought to fields and villages possibly from 20 or 30 miles away. Water is so precious in Iran that you should be extremely careful not to damage any "kanat" you may come across.

Wheat bread is the staff of life in Iran. Everywhere you will see people eating round flaps of whole wheat bread—a working man will get away with about 50 pounds of flaps a month.

In the more mountainous part of the country there are about two to three million semi-wandering tribesmen who tend the sheep from which comes the fine wool used in the famous Persian rugs. Because of the lack of grazing land coupled with the severity of the winters, these tribesmen follow the grass through the seasons—in the high upland valleys in the summer and in the lowland ranges in winter.

The majority of people in the cities are handicraft workers—carpenters, shoemakers, bakers, masons, and tailors. Each has a small shop in the bazaar where all the work is done by hand. The rest of the city people are merchants, Government officials, and big landowners. Except for the oil industry (developed and operated by the British with Iranian personnel) and for some recently introduced factories, manufacturing in Iran is still in the handicraft stage.

Hand-woven rugs even today are Iran's most important product. As a matter of fact, many of the modern carpets now made in the United States are woven in old Iranian designs.

The Moslem Religion

UNTIL A few years ago, if a foreigner had attempted to enter a mosque (Moslem church) in Iran, he would probably have been beaten to death, and even today it is safest to keep strictly away from mosques unless you are invited there by a responsible person. At that time the Iranis were among the most fanatical of all Moslems, and the mullahs (priests) were the men who really ran the country. Today, the situation is somewhat changed. The westernization of the country has greatly lessened the power of the mullahs, so that although most Iranis are still very devout, religion is no longer the controlling national force it once was. You will find, generally speaking, that the mullahs hold greater power in the country than in the cities, and that the country people themselves are stronger in their religious beliefs, particularly their distrust of infidels, as they regard any non-Moslem.

At any rate, the Moslem religion is still a force all over the country so that you should know something about it in order to avoid making any bad breaks.

Followers of the Moslem religion believe in one God, Allah, and obey the teachings of his prophet, Mohammed. They follow the religious practices which are set forth in their sacred book, the Koran. Most Moslems are very conscientious about observing carefully the rules of their religion. Here are the five most important rules:

1. Moslems are forbidden to eat pork. To them the pig is an unclean animal. They also believe dogs are unclean. Never

offer pork to a Moslem, and if you have a mascot dog, be sure to keep him away from all Moslems and especially from mosques.

2. The Moslem is forbidden to drink any kind of fermented or distilled liquor. Don't offer him a drink or let him see you drunk. To do either will offend his religious principles.

3. The good Moslem prays five times a day, facing the holy city Mecca in Arabia, kneeling and bowing to the ground no matter where he happens to be when the call to prayer comes. If he starts doing this in your presence, respect his religious sincerity. Do not laugh, but look the other way until he has finished.

4. The Moslem day of rest is Friday. You will find almost all places of business closed.

5. One month during each year all Moslems observe the fast of Ramadan. During that time they do not eat, drink, or smoke between sunrise and sunset, although they may stay up all night to make up for it. This means that they are often irritable at this season, so make allowances. In 1943 Ramadan (Ramazan in Iran) will begin about September 1 and last until about October 1.

Most of the Iranis belong to the Shia sect of the Moslem religion, which differs in some of its beliefs from the Sunni sect to which most of the Moslems of other countries belong. This probably won't make much difference in your relations with the Iranis, but it might come in handy to know about it. In the past the Sunni and the Shia sects have fought bloody and bitter wars over their religious differences.

In addition to Ramadan (Ramazan) which both the Shia and Sunni sects observe, the Shias in Iran have a week of mourning called Moharrem even more important to them than Ramadan. During that week the Shias mourn three descendants of the Prophet Mohammed whose deaths in a quarrel over the succession to Mohammed as Caliph of the Moslem religion brought about the split between the two sects. During the week of Moharrem it is a good idea to be especially careful in your dealings with the Iranis. Feeling runs high at that time and in the past many bloody fights have occurred between the Shia Moslems, Sunnis, and nonbelievers.

While Mecca is the holy city of all Moslems, the Shia sect in Iran have a holy city of their own—Meshed, in eastern Iran near the Afghan border. Pilgrims from India and Afghanistan visit the city yearly worshipping at the great "golden mosque," holiest in Iran. Meshed is also the center of education for the mullahs, the religious leaders.

In addition to the Moslems, there are also in Iran small groups of Christians, Jews, and a very ancient religious group, the Zoroastrians. All these religions are recognized officially, a fact which shows that the average inhabitant has a kind of broad tolerance. Respect his religion, and he'll respect yours. That isn't a bad rule at all times. So if somebody takes you to visit a Moslem mosque (and that is the only safe way to go) don't laugh or think it funny that the Moslems keep their hats *on* in church, but take their shoes *off*. They would think our customs just as odd, but would probably be too polite to say so.

Irani Customs And Manners

POLITENESS, AS a matter of fact, is one of the first things you'll notice when you begin to meet the Iranis. Their language is one of the most flowery in the world and one of the richest in polite phrases. They are also very ceremonious. There is no back-slapping or rough-housing. And they don't know a thing about boxing or fighting with their fists. If you should happen to lose your temper and knock an Irani down, your outfit would immediately get a bad reputation, to say nothing of the fact that you might run into a mess of trouble sometime later. Personal dignity is very important to an Irani. It is a point to be kept in mind. The natural courtesy of Iranis may be a bit misleading, sometimes. Often you will find that the Iranis you meet will agree with you no matter what you say or will tell you what they think will please you rather than what you really want to know.

Another thing, most of the people are extremely conscious of their long history and their culture, and they believe that Iran is unique among all the nations of the world. There is an old saying in Iran: "Half the World is Isfahan." Isfahan was once one of the most beautiful cities anywhere, and Iranis believed that it took all the rest of the world to equal it. Feeling so, the Iranis probably won't believe any boasting you do about your own country.

Another thing to know in connection with manners is that the Moslem is very modest about exposing his body in the presence of others. Remember this and avoid offending his sense of what is proper and courteous.

Hospitality. The Iranis aren't very prosperous today, but even so they are known for their hospitality, and you may be invited to an Irani home for a meal. In the wealthier homes in the cities the meal is eaten the same way as in the United States. There are tables, chairs, plates, and silverware.

In the poorer homes, however, and in the country the old customs are followed. The best thing to do is to watch your host and do as he does. You probably won't see the women of the family at all. You will sit cross-legged on the floor and eat with your fingers from a tray in the center. *Eat only with your right hand*, even if you are a southpaw. This is a strict custom. Don't eat too much, because what is left is for the women and children.

When you leave you will be expected to shake hands. But do this gently. The Iranis do not have a vice-like grip or pump the hand up and down. If you want to make a gift to your host, some American cigarettes or some form of sweets will be appreciated. Better still, send them along to him later.

When you are in an Irani home don't be too enthusiastic about admiring some particular object. Out of courtesy your host might feel obliged to give it to you. If an Irani makes you a gift, the proper thing to do is to give him one of equal value in return.

Often in a home, or even in a shop, you will be offered coffee or tea. If you don't want any, you may refuse. But if you take one cup or glass, you will be expected to drink at least two and possibly three. To stop at less, once you have started, is considered rude. But do not take a fourth. It may be offered, but you are expected to refuse it. Often the third cup or glass is considered a signal that your visit is at an end and it is time for you to go unless you are quartered in the house.

Irani Women. The position of women in Iran is far more advanced than in many Moslem countries. In the cities the veil has disappeared almost entirely, except on older women, and European dress is becoming the rule. However, you will find that you cannot do in Iran as you would at home. You cannot pick up or date an Irani girl. You must wait for a formal introduction. Even then most Irani girls do not yet have the social life that we are accustomed to. In most homes you will find that the *bee-roon*, or front part of the house, is reserved for men; while the women are in the *andi-roon*, or back part of the house, where no man is allowed to enter or even look in.

Occasionally you will see Irani men and women together in public, but most social life is still for men only. You will never see a man and woman walking arm in arm. On the other hand, you will frequently see men walking hand in hand. Don't let this give you any funny ideas about them. It is simply the way of expressing friendship.

Any approach you might make to an Irani woman, either in the country or the city, would be sure to be resented and would cause almost certain trouble. So keep your distance. Don't make passes. Don't even stare at the women. To do this would only cause trouble, and anyway it won't get you anywhere.

Bargaining. Most tradesmen have stalls in the bazaars, which you will find in all the cities, and bargaining is a great national pastime. You will have to bargain for almost everything you buy. The price first quoted is always higher than you should pay. A little good-natured American horse trading will get the price down anywhere from a third to two-thirds. However, you must expect to pay more for things than the Iranis do. As an American soldier, you are paid as much in a month as many natives earn in half a year or more, and they will think it only fair that you should pay higher prices.

Language. There is really no single language in Iran. The language you will hear will depend on the part of the country you are in. In the north, many of the people speak a form of Turkish. Near the Persian Gulf in the south, you will hear Arabic. There are numerous other languages and dialects, and many of the educated Iranians speak French and English. However, the official language of the country is known as Farsee, or, more commonly, Persian, and nearly all Iranis understand some of it. Study the Farsee words and phrases at the end of this guide, and use them, and you will be able to get along.

You should particularly learn some of the most common polite phrases of greeting, parting, etc., such as: *sa-LAH-mun a-LAY-kum* (Peace be on you) which is used in greeting;

KHOO-da HAH-fiz (God be your Protector) which is said when taking leave of someone; *bis-MIL-lah* (In the name of God) which is said before eating; and *mam-NOON-am*, which is one of the many ways of saying "Thank you."

Remember again: your cue is to be polite but not familiar.

Sports and Amusements. Except in Teheran, you won't find movies or hot spots, and you'll depend on what sports equipment your outfit brings with it for amusement. There is, however, good hunting and some fishing. Iran has plenty of quail, snipe, and woodcock, and you'll find wild boar in some sections. If you are out after the latter don't make the mistake of blasting away at him with an ordinary shot gun. The bullets will bounce off his tough hide and he'll probably run you all the way back to camp—if you can keep ahead of him.

Another favorite sport is chasing gazelle in a jeep. The main difficulty is to catch up with them, for the gazelle is almost as swift and shifty as our own western antelope. Also, you'd better watch out for chuck holes during the chase.

The Iranis have a novel, and ancient, way of catching ducks worth trying. You'll need a large flashlight, a piece of net rigged like a butterfly net, a dishpan, and a club. Plant yourself in the reeds at night, turn on the flashlight, bang on the dishpan with your club, and scoop up the duck in the net when he flies down at the light. It's not as easy as it sounds and more fun than banging away with a gun.

INSTRUCTIONS FOR AMERICAN SERVICEMEN IN IRAN DURING WORLD WAR II

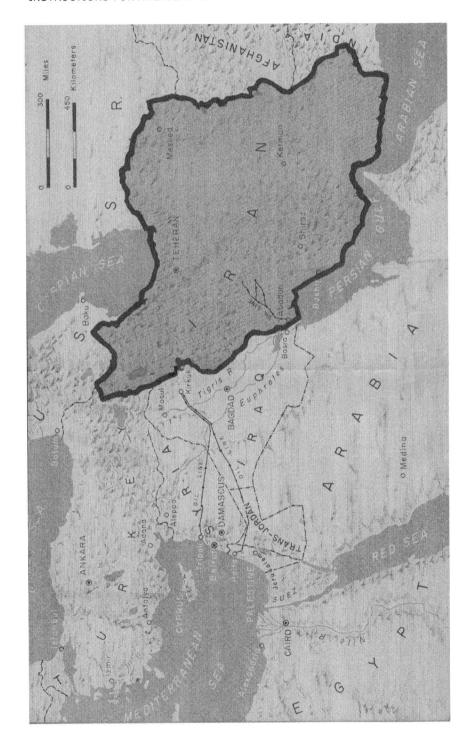

Land Of Iran

THE KINGDOM of Iran occupies the western two-thirds of the great Iranian plateau that stretches across southwestern Asia from the Indus River in India to the Tigris in Iraq. Iran itself extends roughly 600 miles from the Caspian Sea on the north to the Persian Gulf on the south; about 900 miles from Afghanistan and Baluchistan on the east to Turkey and Iraq on the west. It has an area equal to about one-fifth that of the United States—628,000 square miles—with a population about one-tenth as great as ours.

Most of the country is tableland, ranging in elevation from 3,000 to 8,000 feet above sea level; but there are two areas of coastal lowlands. The one along the shores of the Persian Gulf is a desert with very hot dry winds. The other, bordering the Caspian Sea, is hot and wet, with tropical jungles where there are tigers to be hunted. At the edges of the tableland are ranges of mountains which resemble our Rockies. To cross these mountains the Trans-Iranian Railway requires 224 tunnels and 4,102 bridges in the course of its 870 miles from the Persian Gulf to the Caspian Sea.

The greater part of the tableland where most of the people live is desert—much like the drier regions of western United States. In the summer, the countryside is brown and desolate, and in the eastern part are such areas as the Dasht-i-Kavir (salt desert) and the Lut Desert, which are absolutely barren. Very few people live in this eastern part of the tableland. Those who do make their living as shepherds. In the western portion there are mountain ranges and high valleys. Here, wherever water is available, there is irrigation farming much like that practiced in Utah and Nevada.

The large cities are located in the irrigated spots. Teheran, the capital, has a population of more than 300,000. Tabriz, in the northwest corner, has about 220,000 people; Isfahan, in the western mountains, 100,000; Meshed, in the eastern mountains, 140,000; and Resht, on the rainy Caspian coast, about 90,000. Some of these cities are very interesting for their architecture and people, while Teheran is modern in many respects though you will not find the kind of entertainment to which you are accustomed at home.

The climate of Iran is healthful, except in the Caspian lowlands, where malarial mosquitoes are a danger. On the tableland the weather resembles that of Iowa, Nebraska, and the Dakotas though there is less rainfall. In winter temperatures are low, although they seldom drop below zero. In summer, they average between 70 and 90 degrees, sometimes soaring above 100. On the tableland, even when the days are hot, be prepared for sudden drops in temperature after the sun goes down.

Everywhere, except along the northern coast, rainfall is scanty. On the eastern tableland the rain seldom exceeds eight inches annually, and the western tableland averages 15 inches—about the same as Salt Lake City.

History And Government

TWO THOUSAND five hundred years ago, Iran, then Persia, was the military nation of the world. Cyrus the Great, the first of a series of soldier kings, established an empire that included the whole of the Middle East from India to the Mediterranean and from the Caucasus Range to the Indian Ocean.

In those early years as a world empire, Iran was organized for total war. According to military historians it was the first nation to set up a system of universal military service. Boys of five began training in the use of arms and at the age of 15 entered into a 5-year period of advanced training. After that they were reservists, liable for military duty when needed, until they reached the age of 50.

The Persians were also believed to have been the first to employ archers on a large scale to increase the firepower of their forces. And they developed this arm further by putting the bowmen on horseback.

Darius the First, grandson of Cyrus, was noted particularly for his attention to the problems of supply. One of his major works was the construction of a vast network of military roads over which troops and supplies could be transported to any threatened part of the empire. He also established an empire-wide system of communication by mounted carriers—not unlike the famous Pony Express in America 80 years ago.

In 331 B.C., the Iranian Empire was finally overthrown by Alexander the Great at the Battle of Arbela. With about 47,000 men, he defeated more than a million Persians under

Darius III. In this decisive battle, the Persians used elephants, probably the first time in history that they appeared on a battlefield as offensive weapons, their tactical employment being quite like that of the tank in today's warfare.

It took 500 years for Iran to make a come-back as a nation. Then, under Ardashir, a tribal chief, the people reconquered much of their old empire in the Middle East and again drove into India. For the next 400 years, the Persians were constantly at war, fighting about 15 major wars with the Roman Empire and numerous smaller ones with the White Huns, the Arabs, the Turks, and the Khazars.

In the 11th century, Iran, along with other countries, suffered one of the worst blitzkriegs in history. Hordes of Mongol horsemen, capable of traveling 80 miles a day or 1,000 miles a month, swept out of the East, destroying everything in their path. At Merv, a city in the north-western part of the empire, 500,000 people were killed. At Nishapur, all things living, even the animals, were wiped out, and the city was leveled. For the next 100 years, the country—what there was left of it—was ruled by the descendants of the Mongol conquerors.

Split into small states and dominated by foreign rulers for several hundred years, Persia arose again in the 16th century under the Safavid kings, the greatest of which was Shah Abbas. Partially under the heel of Turkey, whose military power was nearly at its height, Shah Abbas began the reorganization of the Persian Army which was then composed almost exclusively of light cavalry. With the help of two British soldier-adventurers, the Shirleys, a well-equipped army of cavalry, infantry, and artillery divisions was created. In its first major trial, the new army met and defeated a superior Turkish force, inflicting more than 20,000 casualties.

From the 17th century on, the history of Iran was one of increasing foreign influence, with England and Russia the predominant nations. Wars and internal strife were almost incessant so that by the time the First World War broke out Iran was almost in a state of anarchy. During the war the British, Russians, and Turks occupied parts of the country. In 1921 a new leader, Reza Khan, arose, an officer in the famous Cossack Division, later to become Shah. Under his leadership many steps toward modernization of the country were taken.

In August 1941 he abdicated in favor of his son, Mohammed Riza Shah.

Today Iran is a constitutional monarchy, with a Shah and a parliament which is elected every 2 years. Iranian politics are in a somewhat delicate state due to the war situation, so it is important that you avoid any expression of opinion on political matters.

Sanitary Conditions

YOU WILL find few of the sanitary precautions which you take for granted at home. Even in the capital, Teheran, which the Iranians consider the most beautiful capital in the world, and which has wide streets and modern buildings, you will find no central water supply and no sewerage system.

In the cities, most of the toilets are crude outhouses. In the villages there are not even these, and you will have to get used to relieving yourself outdoors at any convenient and secluded spot. In both the cities and the country you will have to carry your own supply of toilet paper.

Because of the lack of sewage disposal, you must *never drink any water that has not been boiled*. The open irrigation ditches are so full of germs it is not even safe to wash in them. The best drink is hot tea. Ices (sherbets) are no safer than the water from which they are made, and in general should be avoided.

Malaria is carried by mosquitoes, and mosquito nets are a necessity wherever these insects are found. The nets will also help to protect you from scorpions, which look a bit like crayfish and which have a painful and sometimes dangerous sting. They like to sleep in shoes, so be sure to shake yours out in the morning before you put them on.

Skin, scalp, and eye diseases are common, so personal cleanliness is very important. Be careful, too, never to rub your eyes. Venereal disease is prevalent. Don't take chances!

These are some general health hints. Your medical and sanitary officers will give you more detailed instructions.

Miscellaneous Information

CURRENCY. The principal unit of currency in Iran is the rial (pronounced "ree-AHL"). It is worth about three cents in American money, and is also worth 100 dinars ("DEE-nar"), just as the American dollar is worth 100 cents. There is no coin for a single dinar, however. The smallest Irani coin is an aluminum or bronze piece worth five dinars. Other coins are 10, 25, 50 dinar pieces; and 1, 2, and 5 rial silver, coins. The officers of your outfit will very likely make arrangements for you to change your money into Iranian currency. If you change your own, however, better go to a reputable bank. The rate of exchange varies constantly, and the professional money changers are quick to take advantage of your ignorance of exchange rates.

Calendar. In Iran the Government and most business houses follow a calendar peculiar to Iran. Their New Year's Day, called No Rooz, is the 21st of March. There are 12 months of 30 or 31 days each starting from that date. The "lunar" or "moon" calendar is used by religious groups. That means that there are 13 months of 28 days each. It also means that special dates will not occur at the same time of the year as on our calendar. For instance, in 1942, the feast of Ramadan began about September 10, but in 1943 the date falls around September 1. All religious holidays are figured by the lunar calendar, and thus vary from year to year.

Time. Train schedules and government offices use the 24-hour clock, which is the same as our official Army time. On this clock 1 p.m. ordinary times becomes 13 o'clock, 6 p.m. is 18 o'clock, 11 p.m. is 23 o'clock, etc. Outside of the cities, the Moslems are very vague about the time, and generally use sunrise and sunset as a standard. In fact, time does not have a great deal of meaning to the Iranis. Speed and haste are almost unknown. When an Irani says "now" he means within an hour or so. When he says "tomorrow" (FAR-DAH) frequently he means sometime in the future.

Black Tents of the KASHGAI

Weights and Measures. The metric system is used for all official measurement and weights in Iran. The unit of length in the metric system is the "meter," which is 39.37 inches, or a little more than one of our yards. The unit of road distance is the "kilometer," which is 1,000 meters or about five-eighths (a little over one-half) of one of our miles. The unit of weight is the "kilogram," which equals 2.2 pounds in our system. Liquids are measured by the "liter," which is a little more than one of our quarts.

However, the Iranis have several local systems of weights and measures of their own. If you run into any of these you will simply have to learn them when the time comes.

In rural districts, particularly, the Iranis are as vague about distances as they are about time. They have traveled very little and do not know distances. Do not place too much confidence in anything they tell you.

Check List Of Do's And Don'ts

Respect the Iranis as men and as soldiers; recognize that their way of life is as right and natural for them as yours is for you.

Expect to bargain for your purchases and always arrive at a price before accepting any goods or services whatsoever.

Always wash your hands before eating, and say *"Bismillah"* if Moslems are present.

Respect the Moslems at prayer.

Keep any dogs of your own away from mosques and from Moslem homes.

Drink water only as hot tea or after boiling.

In general, take your cues on manners from the Iranis and remember that your mission may fail if you make enemies of them.

Don't try to tell Iranis how much better everything is in the United States. They think most things are better in Iran.

Don't discuss religion.

Don't discuss politics.

Don't enter mosques unless you are invited and escorted there by a Moslem.

Don't offer an Irani liquor or drink it in front of him.

Don't offer an Irani pork in any form: bacon, sausage, or food cooked in lard.

Don't touch or jostle Irani men; even those you know quite well will resent it.

Don't touch a respectable Irani woman, or even look at one unnecessarily.

Don't strike an Irani.

Don't threaten Iranis; use persuasion, explanation, and rewards to get things done.

Don't expose your body in the presence of an Irani.

Don't mistake courtesy for friendship; an Irani is always polite, but he is fundamentally suspicious of foreigners.

Don't expect definite future commitments; when an Irani says "now" he means "this very hour"; when he says FAR-DAH (tomorrow) he means "sometime in the future."

Don't expect definite knowledge of distances from country men; they travel little and have never learned to use numbers (except very small ones) with any exactness.

Don't ridicule or criticize the Iranis in English in public places. Some know English quite as well as you do.

Above all, use common sense on all occasions. And remember that every American soldier is an unofficial ambassador of good will.

Hints On Pronouncing Persian

THESE ARE pronunciation hints to help you in listening to the Persian language records which have been supplied to your troop unit. They will also help you with the pronunciation of additional words and phrases given in the vocabulary below, which are not included in the records.

There is nothing very difficult about Persian—except that you won't be able to read signs and newspapers you will see. That is because the Persians use a different alphabet from ours. Therefore, the instructions and vocabulary below are not based on the written Persian language, but are a simplified system of representing the language as it *sounds*. This system contains letters for all the sounds you *must* make to be understood. It does *not* contain letters for some of the sounds you will hear, but it will give you enough to get by on, both listening and speaking. The sounds of Persian vary from region to region, very much as English varies in pronunciation in this country. The dialect you will hear on the records is a northern dialect, and if you follow it you will be understood almost everywhere.

Here are a few simple rules to help you:

1. *Accents*. You know what the accented syllable of a word is, of course. It is the syllable which is spoken louder than the other syllables in the same word. We will show accented (loud) syllables in capital letters and unaccented syllables in small letters.

2. *Vowels*. These are the kind of sounds we represent in English by *a, e, i, o, u, ah, ay,* etc. Just follow the key below and you will have no trouble.

a or A	equals	the *a* in *pat* (Example: *NA* meaning "no")
ah or AH	equals	the *a* in *father* (Example: *CHAHR*, meaning "four")
ay or AY	equals	the *ay* in *day* (Example: *sa-LAH-mun a-LAY-kum*, meaning "good day")
e or E	equals	the *e* in *pet* (Example: *YEK*, meaning "one")
ee or EE	equals	the *ee* in *feet* (Example: *BEEST* meaning "twenty")
i or I	equals	the *i* in *pit* (Example: *IS-mi* meaning "my name is")
aw or AW	equals	the *aw* in *awful* but clipped short (Example: *jawm-E* meaning "Friday")
oo or OO	equals	the *oo* in *boot* (Example: *mam-NOON-am* meaning "thank you")
u or U	equals	the *u* in *put* (Example: *khah-NUM*, mean-ing "Madam or Miss")
o or O	equals	the *o* in *note* (Example: *AHB-e JO* meaning "beer")

3. *Consonants*. The consonants are all the sounds that are not vowels. Pronounce them just as you know them in English. *All consonants should be pronounced. Never "slight" them.* Here are some special consonant sounds to learn.

h	small *h* is always pronounced with the *h* sound except after *a*. Listen carefully to the *h* sound on the records
kh	is pronounced as when clearing your throat when you have to spit. Listen carefully for it on the records

gh   is pronounced like *kh* except it is not so strong and you put your "voice" into it. That is, a sound very much like a gentle gargle. Listen carefully to this sound on the records

sh   is like the *sh* in *show*

ch   is like the *ch* in *church*

zh   is like the *z* in *azure* or the *s* in *measure*

ng   is like the *ng* in *sing*

List Of Most Useful Words And Phrases

HERE IS a list of the most useful words and phrases you will need in Persian. *You should learn these by heart.* They are the words and phrases included on the Persian language records, and appear here in the order they occur on the records.

Greetings and General Phrases
[English—*Simplified Arabic Spelling*]

Good day — *sa-LAH-mun a-LAY-kum*
Sir — *AH-ghah*
Madam — *khah-NUM*
Miss — *khah-NUM*
Please — *khah-HESH MEE-kaw-nam*
Excuse me — *BE-bakh-sheed*
Thank you — *mam- NOON-am*

Yes — *BA-le*
No — *NA*
Understand me? — *MA-RAh MEE-fa-meed*
I don't understand — *NA-mee-fa-mam*
Please, speak slowly — *khah-HISH MEE-kaw-nam, aw-hes-TE HARFBE-za-NEED*

INSTRUCTIONS FOR AMERICAN SERVICEMEN IN IRAN DURING WORLD WAR II

Location

Where is — kaw-JAHST
a hotel — MEH-mahng-khah-NE
Where is a hotel? — MEH-mahng-khah-NE kaw-JAHST
a restaurant — rest-RAHN
Where is a restaurant? — rest-RAHN kaw-JAHST
railroad station — EEST-i GAHh
Where is a railroad station? — EEST-i GAHh kaw-JAHST
a toilet — ma-BAHL
Where is a toilet? — ma-BAHL kaw-JAHST

Directions

turn right — be RAHST BE-pee-cheed
turn left — be CHAP BE-pee-cheed
go straight ahead — RAHST BE-ra-veed
please point — khah-HISH MEE-kaw-nam, mi-SHAHN BE-de-heed

Distances are given in kilometers, not miles.
One kilometer equals 5/8 of a mile.
kilometers — ki-lo-METR

Numbers

one — YEK
two — DAW
three — SE
four — CHAHR
five — PANJ
six — SHISH
seven — HAFT
eight — HASHT
nine — NAWh
ten — DAh
eleven — yahz-DAh
twelve — da-vahz-DAh
thirteen — seez-DAh
fourteen — chahr-DAh
fifteen — pahnz-DAh
sixteen — shahnz-DAh
seventeen — heev-DAh
eighteen — heej-DAh

nineteen — nooz-DAh
twenty — BEEST
twenty-one — BEEST-aw-YEK
thirty — SEE
thirty-two — SEE-aw-DO
forty — che-HIL
fifty — pan-JAHh

sixty — SHAST
seventy — haf-TAHD
eighty — hash-TAHD
ninety — na-VAD
one hundred — SAD
a thousand — he-ZAHR

Designations

What is — CHEEST
this — IN
What's this? — IN CHEEST
I — MAN
cigarettes — si-GAHR
want — MEE-khahm

I want cigarettes — MAN si-GAHR MEE-khahm
to eat — BE-khaw-ram
I want to eat — MAN MEE-khawm BE-khaw-ram

Food

Bread — NAHN
Fruit — mee-VE
Water — AHB
Eggs — TAWKH-me MAWRGH
Meat — GUSHT
Potatoes — SEEB-e za-mee-NEE
Rice dish — pi-LO
Beans — loo-bee-YAH
Fish — mah-HEE

Milk — SHEER
Beer — AHB-e JO
A glass of beer — YEK gi-LAHS AHB-e JO
A cup of coffee — YEK fin-JAHN GAh-VE
A cup of tea — YEK fin-JAHN chah-EE

To find out how much things cost you say:
How much? — CHAND

Money

One "ree-AHL" — YEK ree-AHL   Two "ree-AHL" — DAW ree-AHL

Time

What time is it? — sah-AT CHAND ast
Ten past one — DAh da-gee-GE AZ YEK gaw-zash-TE
Quarter past five — YEK RAWB AZ PANJ gaw-zash-TE
Twenty past seven — BEEST da-gee-GE AZ HAFT gaw-zash-TE
Half past six — SHISH-aw NEEM
Twenty of eight — BEEST da-gee-GE be HASHT MEE-mah-nad
Quarter of two — YEK RAWB be DAW MEE-mah-nad

What time — CHE VAKHT
the movie — see-na-MAH
starts — shaw-ROO MEE-sha-vad
At what time does the movie start? — CHE VAKHT see-na-MAH shaw-ROO MEE-sha-vad
the train — mah-SHIN
leave — ha-ra-KAT MEE-kaw-nad
What time does the train leave? — CHE VAKHT mah-SHIN ha-ra-KAT MEE-kaw-nad
Today — IM-ROOZ
Tomorrow — FAR-DAH

Days of the Week

Sunday — YEK-sham-BE
Monday—DAW-sham-BE
Tuesday — SE-sham-BE
Wednesday — CHAHR-sham-BE

Thursday—PANJ-sham-BE
Friday — jawm-E
Saturday — sham-BE

Useful Phrases

What is your name? — IS-mi shaw-MAH CHEEST
My name is John — IS-mi MAN John ast

How do you say "table" in Persian? — DAR fahr-SEE table CHE MEE-goo-eed
Goodbye — khaw-DAH hah-FEZ

Surroundings—Natural Objects

bank (of a river) — aw-HEL
darkness—TAH-ree-KEE
daytime (light) — ROOZ
desert — SAh-RAH or bee-ah-BAHN
fire — ah-TASH
forest or jungle — jan-GAL
woods or grove — bee-SHE
grass — a-LAF
ground — za-MEEN
hill — ta-PE
ice — YAKH

lake — DAR-yah-CHE
mountain — KOOH
ocean — dar-YAH
rain — bah-PAHN
river — ROOD khan-NE
snow — BARF
spring or water-hole — CHEYSH-ME
stars — se-tah-RE
stream — ROOD
sun — ahf-TAHB
wind — BAHD

Time

day — ROOZ
day after tomorrow — pas-far-DAH
day before yesterday — pa-ree-ROOZ
yesterday — dee-ROOZ

evening—av-VAL-e SI-IAB
month — MAHh
night — SHAB
week — haf-TE
year — SAHL

Persian Months

March 21 to April 21 — far-var-DEEN
April 21 to May 21 — or-dee-be-HISHT
May 21 to June 21 — khor-DAHD
June 21 to July 21 — TEER
July 21 to August 21 — mor-DAHD
August 21 to September 21 — SHAh-ree-VAR
September 21 to October 21 — MEhR
October 21 to November 21 — ah-BAHN
November 21 to December 21 — ah-ZAR
December 21 to January 21 — DAY
January 21 to February 21 — BAh-MAN
February 21 to March 21 — is-FAND

Relationships

boy (or son) — pe-SAR
brother — ba-rah-DAR
child — ba-CHE
daughter (or girl) — dukh-TAR
family — KHAH-ne-vah-DE
father — pe-DAR
husband — sho-HAR
man — MARD
mother — mah-DAR
sister — khah-HAR
woman — ZAN

Human Body

arm — bah-ZOO
back — PAWSHT
body — ba-DAN
ear — GOOSH
hand — DAST
head — SAR
leg — SAHGH-e PAH
mouth — da-HAN
neck — gar-DAN
eye — CHESHM
finger — ang-GAWSHT
foot — PAH
hair — MOO
nose — da-MAHGH or bee-NEE
teeth — dan-dah-HAH
thigh — RAHN
toe — ang-GAWSHT-e PAH

House and Furniture

bed — TAKH-te KHAHB
blanket — pa-TOO
chair — san-da-LEE
door — DAR
room — aw-TAHGH
stairs — pil-la-KAWN
stove (cooking place) — baw-kha-REE
table — MEEZ

house — khah-NE
kitchen — AHSH-paz khah-NE
mosquito net — pa-sheh-BAND
quilt — la-HAHF
wall — dee-VAHR
water for washing — AHB-e shaws-taw-SHOO
window — pan-ja-RE

Food and Drink—Tobacco

cabbage — ka-LAM
cauliflower — GAWL-e ka-LAM
cucumbers — khee-YAHR
food — khaw-RAHK
grapes — an-GOOR
lemons — lee-MOO
watermelon — hen-de-vah-NE
honeydew melon — khar-bi-ZE
oranges — por-te-GHAHL

pipe — se-BEEL
radishes — taw-rawb-CHE
salt — na-MAK
sugar — she-KAR
tobacco — tu-TUN
tomatoes — GO-je fa-ran-GEE
turnip — shal-GHAM
wine — sha-RAHB

Surroundings

bridge — PAWL
church — ka-lee-SAH
mosque — mas-JED
path — RAHh
post-office — POST khaw-NE
police post — ka-lahn-ta-REE
road — RAHh

city or town — SHAhR
market place — bah-ZAHR
shop (store) — dawk-KAWN
street — koo-CHE
village — DEh
well — CHAHh

Animals

animal — hay-VAHN
bird — pa-ran-DE
camel — shaw-TAWR
chicken (hen) — ju-JE
cow — GAHV
dog — SAG
donkey — ow-LAHGH
goat — BAWZ

horse — ASB
mouse or rat — MOOSH
mule — kah-TER
rabbit — khar-GOOSH
sheep — goos-FAND
snake — MAHR
scorpion — agh-RAB

Insects

ants — MOOR or moor-CHE
flies — ma-GAS
fleas — KAK
mosquitoes — pa-SHE

lice — she-PESH
spider — an-ka-BOOT
bedbugs — SAHS

Trades and Occupations

baker — NAHN-VAH
barber — sal-mah-NEE
blacksmith — ah-han-GAR
butcher — ghas-SAHB
cook — ahsh-PAZ
doctor — pe-ZEZHG
farmer — zah-RE

mechanic — me-kah-NEEK
policeman — pahs-BAHN
servant — no-KAR
shoemaker — kaf-FAHSH
tailor — khay-YAHT

Clothing

belt — ka-mar-BAND
boots — chak-ME
coat — KAWT
shirt — pee-rah-HAN
shoes — KAFSH
socks — joo-RAHB

gloves — dast-KESH
hat — kaw-LAHh
necktie — ka-rah-VAHT
trousers — shal-VAHR
undershirt — ZEER pee-rah-ha-NEE

Adjectives

good — KHOOB
bad — BAD
big, large, great — baw-ZAWRG
small or little — koo-CHEK
right — RAHST
left — CHAP
sick — nah-KAWSH
well — KHOOB or KHAWSH
hungry — gaw-raws-NE
thirsty — tesh-NE
black — see-YAHh
white — sa-FEED
red — SAWRKH
blue — ah-BEE
green — SABZ
yellow — ZARD
high — baw-LAND
low — koo-TAHh
deep — GOD or a-MEEGH
shallow — GOD NEEST
cold — SARD
hot — GARM
wet — TAR

dry — KHAWSHK
expensive — ge-RAHN
cheap — ar-ZAHN
empty — khah-LEE
full — PAWR
long — de-RAHZ
short — koo-TAHh
heavy — san-GEEN
light — sa-BAWK
old (of persons) — PEER
old (of things) — kawh-NE
new — NO
young — ja-VAHN
clean — PAHK
dirty — ka-SEEF
far — DOOR
near — naz-DEEK
North — she-MAHL
South — jaw-NOOB
East — SHARGH
West — GHARB

Pronouns, etc.

we — MAH
you — shaw-MAH
he — OO
she — OO
they — awn-HAH
these — in-HAH
those — awn-HAH

who — KEE
what — CHE
how many — chand-TAH
how far — CHE GHADR RAH-hast
anyone — KA-see
everybody — HAR-kas

Prepositions

for — ba-RAH-ye
from — AZ
in — DAR or TOO ye

on — ROO-ye
to or up to — BE
with — BAH

Adverbs

above — BAH-LAH
again — daw-bah-RE
behind — PAWSHT
below — pah-EEN
far — DOOR
here — in-JAH
in front — je-LO

less — KAM
more — zee-AHD
near — naz-DEEK
on that side — da-RAWN-ta-raf
on this side — da-RIN-ta-raf
there — awn-JAH
very — KHAY-lee

Conjunctions

and — VA
but — VA-lee

if — a-GAR
or — YAH

Phrases for Every Day

What date is today? — EM-rooz CHAND DOM-e MAH-hast
What day of the week? — EM-rooz CHE ROO-zeest
Today is the fifth of June — EM-rooz PAN-jaw-me MAW-he JOO-ne
Today is Tuesday, etc. — EM-rooz se-sham-BAST
Come here — BEE-ah in-JAH
Come quickly — ZOOD BEE-ah eed
Go quickly — ZOOD BE-ra-veed
Who are you? — shaw-MAH KEES-teed
What do you want? — CHE MEE-khan-heed
Bring some drinking water — GHAD-ree AHB-e khawr-da-NEE BEE-ah-reed
Bring some food — GHAD-ree khaw-RAHK BEE-ah-reed
How far is the camp? — be awr-di GAHh CHE GHADR RAH-hast
How far is the water? — be AHB CHE GHADR RAH-hast
Whose house is this? — in khah-NE-ye KEEST
Where is the nearest village? — naz-DEEK-ta-REEN DEh kaw-JAHST
Danger! — kha-TAR
Stop! — EEST
Wait a minute — KA-mee SABR kaw-NEED
Where is a place to sleep? — JAH-ye khah-bee-DAN kaw-JAHST
I haven't any money — MAN HEETCH POOL NA-dah-ram
I have cigarettes — MAN soc-GAHR dah-RAM
I am sick — MAN nah-KHAWSH HAS-tam
I am an American — MAN see-ree-kah-EE HAS-tam
I am your friend — MAN DOOS-te shaw-MAH HAS-tam

Works Cited

Limbert, John W. *Negotiating With Iran: Wrestling the Ghosts of History*. Washington, DC: United States Institute of Peace Press, 2009.

Motter, T.H.Vail. *The Persian Corridor and Aid to Russia. U.S. Army in World War II Series*. Washington, DC: Center of Military History, 1952.

Sayre, Joel. *Persian Gulf Command: Some Marvels on the Road to Kazvin*. New York: Random House, 1945.

Ward, Steven R. *Immortal: A Military History of Iran and Its Armed Forces*. Washington, DC: Georgetown University Press, 2009.

About the Author

Steven R. Ward is a senior CIA intelligence analyst who specializes in Iran and the Middle East. He recently was a Visiting Professor to the US Naval Academy at Annapolis. From 2005 to 2006 he served as the Deputy National Intelligence Officer for the Near East on the National Intelligence Council, and he served on the National Security Council from 1998 to 1999. He also is a graduate of the US Military Academy at West Point and a retired U.S. Army Reserve lieutenant colonel.

Made in the USA
Lexington, KY
30 April 2012